52 WEEKS

MINISTRY
OF THE

DEVOTIONAL

52 WEEKS MINISTRY OF THE WIFE DEVOTIONAL

Copyright © 2025 by Douglas Asante

All rights reserved. No portion of this book may be reproduced, stored in a retrieval system, or transmitted in any form or by any means - electronic, mechanical, photocopy, recording, scanning, or other - except for brief quotations in critical reviews or articles, without the prior written permission of the publisher.

ISBN: 978-1-916692-38-1

Email the author via **info@dasante.org.uk**
Visit the website for more information: **www.dasante.org.uk**

Published in the United Kingdom by
Equip Publishing House

DEDICATION

To every wife who seeks to honour God in her marriage,

To the women who rise daily to nurture, love, and strengthen their families,

And to those who quietly pour out prayers for their husbands and children—this devotional is dedicated to you.

May you find encouragement, wisdom, and renewed strength as you embrace the beautiful ministry God has entrusted to you as a wife. May your marriage become a living testimony of Christ's love and faithfulness.

With love and prayers,

Douglas

CONTENTS

Dedication iii
Preface vii
Introduction ix
Reader's Guide: How to Use This Devotional xi

Part I – The Wife's Identity and Calling

Created in God's Image 1
The Wife as a Helper Fit 3
The Beauty of Partnership 5
Marriage as Covenant 7
The Wife's Crown of Wisdom 9
Respect that Revives: Honouring with Grace 11
The Wife's Quiet Strength 13
The Wife's Influence 15
Strength in Submission 17
The Wife's Prayer Power 19
Hospitality from the Heart: Making Room for Grace 21
The Wife's Tongue 23
Faith that Stands: Trusting God Through Every Season 25

Part II – The Wife's Nurturing Ministry

The Wife's Diligence 27
The Wife's Joy 29
The Wife's Endurance 31
The Wife's Nurturing Heart 33
The Wife's Stewardship 35
The Wife's Encouragement 37
The Wife's Generosity 39
Compassion that Heals: Reflecting Christ's Tender Heart 41
The Wife's Hope 43
The Wife's Faithfulness 45
Gratitude in Every Season: Seeing God's Hand 47

Wisdom that Builds: Guiding with Discernment and Grace 49

The Peacemaker's Presence: Cultivating Calm at Home 51

The Wife's Respect 53

Part III – The Wife's Inner Growth

The Wife's Courage 55

The Wife's Service 57

Forgiveness that Frees: Healing Through Grace 59

Patience Perfected: Waiting with Faith and Love 61

The Wife's Prayer 63

The Wife's Hospitality 65

The Wife's Humility 67

The Wife's Perseverance 69

The Wife's Faith 71

The Wife's Kindness 73

The Wife's Joy 75

The Wife's Integrity 77

The Wife's Obedience 79

The Wife's Gratitude 81

The Wife's Hope 83

The Wife's Faithfulness 85

The Wife's Love 87

Part IV – The Wife's Legacy

The Wife's Peace 89

The Wife's Wisdom 91

The Wife's Contentment 93

The Wife's Strength 95

The Wife's Patience 97

The Wife's Compassion 99

The Wife's Forgiveness 101

The Wife's Devotion 103

PREFACE

When I first began reflecting on the sacred role of a wife, I realised how often the world's voice competes with God's design. Marriage is not merely a partnership of convenience but a covenant shaped by grace, sacrifice, and love. In that covenant, the ministry of the wife is both profound and powerful—a calling to nurture, encourage, and support, while reflecting Christ in everyday life.

This devotional was born out of prayer and a deep desire to encourage wives in their journey. I have witnessed, both in Scripture and in real life, the immeasurable impact a godly wife can have on her husband, children, and community. Her ministry is not confined to household duties or external achievements; it flows from her walk with God, her character shaped by His Spirit, and her willingness to serve in love.

My hope is that these weekly reflections will not feel like another task to add to an already full life, but rather a source of renewal and strength. Each week offers Scripture, insight, and practical steps designed to help you embrace God's Word in the ordinary and extraordinary moments of marriage.

You may be in a season of joy, or perhaps walking through difficulty. Wherever you find yourself, know this: God sees you, God is with you, and God delights in working through you. Your ministry as a wife is unique and valuable, and when surrendered to Him, it becomes a testimony of His love and faithfulness.

It is my prayer that as you journey through these 52 weeks, you will not only grow in your role as a wife but also deepen your identity as a beloved daughter of God. May this devotional remind you that the most significant ministry begins at home and flows outward to bless the world.

With humility and gratitude,

DOUGLAS

INTRODUCTION

Marriage is one of God's most beautiful gifts to humanity. From the very beginning, when God created Eve as a helper suitable for Adam, He established marriage as a covenant designed to reflect His love, unity, and faithfulness (Genesis 2:18–24; Ephesians 5:31–32). Within this sacred covenant, the ministry of the wife holds a special and irreplaceable role.

This devotional, *52 Weeks Ministry of the Wife Devotional*, is written to guide wives through a year-long journey of growth, reflection, and prayer. Each week provides Scripture, thoughtful teaching, and practical application—inviting wives to deepen their walk with God and to strengthen the spiritual, emotional, and relational foundations of their marriage.

The purpose of this devotional is not to burden wives with unrealistic expectations, but to encourage them to embrace the grace and wisdom God provides for daily life. It speaks to women in all seasons of marriage—whether newlyweds, mothers, empty nesters, or those walking through challenges. Every wife has a ministry: to love, nurture, support, and build up her family in a way that honours Christ.

Through these 52 weeks, you will explore themes such as love, patience, forgiveness, wisdom, contentment, and devotion. Each reflection is designed to move from understanding God's truth into practical and transformative application. Journaling prompts will help you capture personal insights, while prayers provide words of surrender and faith.

Marriage is not simply about companionship; it is about partnership in God's mission. As you journey through this devotional, may you discover afresh the joy of serving as a wife who reflects Christ's love in her home. And may your marriage grow into a testimony of God's grace and faithfulness—both to those within your household and to the world around you.

Let this be more than a reading plan—make it a rhythm of life. Set aside a few quiet moments each week to dwell in God's Word, reflect on His call, and embrace the ministry He has entrusted to you as a wife.

> *"Unless the Lord builds the house,*
> *they labour in vain who build it."*
>
> PSALM 127:1

READER'S GUIDE: HOW TO USE THIS DEVOTIONAL

This devotional has been designed as a 52-week journey, one reflection for each week of the year. It is not meant to be rushed but embraced slowly, giving God space to transform your heart and marriage step by step.

Structure of Each Week

- SCRIPTURE – A key Bible verse to meditate on throughout the week.
- OBSERVATION – A simple reflection on what the Scripture says.
- INTERPRETATION – Insight into what the passage means and how it relates to marriage.
- CORRELATION – Supporting Bible verses that reinforce the theme.
- APPLICATION – Practical steps you can take in your marriage this week.
- PRAYER – A guided prayer to align your heart with God's will.
- JOURNALING PROMPTS – Questions to help you reflect personally and write down your thoughts.

Suggestions for Weekly Use

1. BEGIN WITH PRAYER – Ask the Holy Spirit to open your heart and guide your reflections.
2. READ THE SCRIPTURE ALOUD – Let God's Word take root in your mind and spirit.

3. **Reflect on the Devotional Sections** – Take your time to process the Observation, Interpretation, and Correlation.

4. **Apply the Word** – Choose at least one Application point to intentionally practice in your marriage during the week.

5. **Pray Daily** – Return to the week's prayer each day, adding your own personal petitions.

6. **Journal** – Use the journaling prompts to record insights, struggles, victories, and answered prayers.

7. **Share Together (Optional)** – If your husband is open, share highlights from your reflection with him to build spiritual intimacy.

Flexibility

This devotional is written for wives individually, but it can also be used:

- *In women's small groups or Bible studies, where wives can encourage one another.*
- *In marriage enrichment groups, where couples study and pray together.*
- *As a personal spiritual rhythm, accompanying your daily Bible reading.*

Remember: this is not about perfection but progress in Christ. Each week builds a deeper foundation of love, faith, and devotion. By the end of 52 weeks, you will not only have grown as a wife but also as a woman of God who ministers to her family with grace and wisdom.

W E E K 1

Created in God's Image

*"So God created man in His own image;
in the image of God He created him;
male and female He created them."*

GENESIS 1:27 (NKJV)

OBSERVATION

From the beginning, God created both man and woman in His image. This was not an afterthought, but a purposeful design. Each carries the likeness of God and together reflect His fullness.

INTERPRETATION

The phrase "in His image" (Hebrew: *tselem*) points to representation — to be God's reflection in the earth. Wives are not merely companions but bearers of God's character. This truth reshapes how we see ourselves: we are not defined by roles, achievements, motherhood, or societal expectations. Instead, we reflect God's nature in how we love, create, nurture, and lead in faith.

CORRELATION

- Psalm 139:14 — I praise You, for I am fearfully and wonderfully made.
- Galatians 3:28 — There is neither male nor female; for you are all one in Christ Jesus.
- 2 Corinthians 3:18 — We are being transformed into the same image from glory to glory.

APPLICATION

Begin your day by thanking God for one attribute of His image reflected in your life.

Ask the Holy Spirit to highlight how you can display God's character in your home.

Prayer

Father, thank You for creating me in Your image. Help me to reflect Your nature in love, wisdom, and strength. Where I have believed lies about my worth, replace them with Your truth. In Jesus' name, Amen.

Journaling Prompts

- *In what ways do I see the image of God expressed in my life and marriage?*
- *Where do I feel inadequate, and what truth from God's Word can I replace it with?*

WEEK 2

The Wife as a Helper Fit

"And the LORD God said, 'It is not good that man should be alone; I will make him a helper comparable to him.'"

GENESIS 2:18 (NKJV)

OBSERVATION

God saw Adam's aloneness and declared it 'not good.' His solution was a wife — not as an inferior, but as a strong helper suitable for him.

INTERPRETATION

The word "helper" (Hebrew: *ezer*) is used in Scripture often of God Himself (e.g., Psalm 121:1–2). It conveys strength, rescue, and support. The wife's role is therefore honourable — she reflects God's own helping nature. Being a 'helper fit' means complementing, strengthening, and standing alongside her husband, not replacing him nor being replaced by him.

CORRELATION

- Ecclesiastes 4:9–10 — Two are better than one, for they have a good return for their labour.
- John 14:16 — The Holy Spirit is our Helper.
- Proverbs 31:11 — The heart of her husband safely trusts her.

APPLICATION

Ask God to show you how you can strengthen your husband this week.

Identify one area where you can bring encouragement or support.

Prayer

Lord, thank You for creating me as a helper fit, reflecting Your own helping nature. Help me to walk in this role with dignity, wisdom, and love. Amen.

Journaling Prompts

- *What misconceptions have I held about being a helper?*
- *How can I practically be a 'fit' help to my husband this week?*

WEEK 3

The Beauty of Partnership

"Two are better than one, because they have a good reward for their labor."

ECCLESIASTES 4:9 (NKJV)

OBSERVATION

Marriage is designed as a partnership — a shared journey where both husband and wife labour together for greater reward.

INTERPRETATION

Partnership implies equality in value and difference in function. Just as the Trinity operates in unity with diversity, so also marriage reflects a divine partnership. When wives embrace partnership, they recognise that their voice, presence, and labour are vital to the success of the marriage.

CORRELATION

- Amos 3:3 — Can two walk together unless they are agreed?
- Matthew 19:6 — What God has joined together, let no one separate.
- Philippians 1:27 — Strive together for the faith of the gospel.

APPLICATION

Initiate one joint activity with your husband this week that strengthens togetherness.

Pray together over one shared goal for your family.

Prayer

Father, thank You for the beauty of partnership. Help my husband and me to labour together in unity, appreciating each other's strengths. Let our marriage reflect Your oneness. Amen.

Journaling Prompts

- *How do I currently view partnership in my marriage?*
- *What practical step can I take to strengthen the partnership this week?*

WEEK 4

Marriage as Covenant

*"Yet she is your companion
and your wife by covenant."*

MALACHI 2:14 (NKJV)

OBSERVATION

Marriage is not merely a contract but a covenant — a binding, sacred promise before God.

INTERPRETATION

Covenant differs from contract. Contracts are based on mutual benefit and can be broken when one side fails to fulfil its obligations. Covenant is based on steadfast commitment and divine witness. As wives, seeing marriage as a covenant shapes how we respond in hard seasons. We do not give up easily, because we are bound by God's design and faithfulness.

CORRELATION

- Ephesians 5:31-32 — Marriage is a picture of Christ and the Church.
- Genesis 15:18 — God Himself makes a covenant as a sign of His faithfulness.
- Matthew 19:6 — What God has joined together, let no man separate.

APPLICATION

Reflect on the vows you made and renew them in prayer.

Identify one way to honour your marriage covenant this week, even in small acts of love.

Prayer

Lord, thank You for covenant. Teach me to honour my marriage as sacred, reflecting Your faithfulness. Strengthen me to live with commitment and grace. Amen.

Journaling Prompts

- *How does viewing marriage as a covenant shape my daily actions?*
- *What areas of my marriage need fresh commitment from me?*

W E E K 5

The Wife's Crown of Wisdom

"An excellent wife is the crown of her husband, but she who causes shame is like rottenness in his bones."

PROVERBS 12:4 (NKJV)

OBSERVATION

A wife is described here as a 'crown' — a visible sign of honour, beauty, and dignity to her husband.

INTERPRETATION

The Hebrew word for crown (*atarah*) symbolises authority, dignity, and celebration. When a wife walks in wisdom and virtue, she becomes her husband's joy and pride. Conversely, foolishness brings harm and dishonour. This imagery calls wives to live as women of wisdom, dignity, and grace, reflecting Christ in their marriages.

CORRELATION

- Proverbs 31:10 — An excellent wife is worth far more than rubies.
- Proverbs 14:1 — A wise woman builds her house.
- Ephesians 5:22 — Wives, submit to your husbands as to the Lord.

APPLICATION

Practice one act of wisdom that builds up your home this week.

Speak words that honour rather than tear down your husband.

PRAYER
Lord, make me a crown of wisdom to my husband. Help me to live with dignity, honour, and grace that reflects You. Amen.

JOURNALING PROMPTS
- *In what ways am I a crown to my husband?*
- *What areas of my speech or actions need God's wisdom?*

WEEK 6

Respect that Revives: Honouring with Grace

"Let the wife see that she respects her husband."

EPHESIANS 5:33

OBSERVATION

Paul joins love and respect as marriage's twin pillars. When a husband loves and a wife honours, their union reflects Christ and His Church.

INTERPRETATION

Respect isn't fear or silence—it's recognising worth. When a wife honours her husband, she breathes life into his heart and faith into their bond. Her words of respect can awaken confidence and healing.

CORRELATION

- Romans 12:10 — Outdo one another in showing honour.
- 1 Peter 3:1–2 — Wives may win their husbands by respectful conduct.
- Proverbs 31:11 — The heart of her husband safely trusts her.

APPLICATION

Speak one word of affirmation daily.

Pray for him where you've been critical.

Let your tone reveal honour even in disagreement.

PRAYER

Lord, teach me to respect my husband with grace. May my words revive love and reflect Your heart. Amen.

JOURNALING PROMPTS

- *How can I show respect today?*
- *What changes when I choose honour over criticism?*

W E E K 7

The Wife's Quiet Strength

"Rather let it be the hidden person of the heart, with the incorruptible beauty of a gentle and quiet spirit, which is very precious in the sight of God."

1 PETER 3:4 (NKJV)

OBSERVATION

Peter reminds wives that true beauty is inward, shaped by a gentle and quiet spirit.

INTERPRETATION

A gentle spirit (*praus*) is strength under control; a quiet spirit (*hesychios*) is peace that trusts in God. These qualities are not weaknesses but deep strengths rooted in faith. Such inner beauty is incorruptible and precious to God. A wife who cultivates this spirit brings peace and stability to her home.

CORRELATION

- Proverbs 31:25 — She is clothed with strength and dignity.
- Isaiah 30:15 — In quietness and trust is your strength.
- Matthew 5:5 — Blessed are the meek, for they shall inherit the earth.

APPLICATION

Take moments of silence this week to centre your heart on God's peace.

Respond with gentleness in one situation where you might normally react harshly.

Prayer

Lord, cultivate in me a gentle and quiet spirit that honours You. Let my inner life reflect Your peace and strength. Amen.

Journaling Prompts

- *What does a gentle and quiet spirit mean for me personally?*
- *How can I nurture inner strength rather than outward appearance?*

WEEK 8

The Wife's Influence

"The wise woman builds her house, but the foolish pulls it down with her hands."

PROVERBS 14:1 (NKJV)

OBSERVATION

This proverb highlights the significant influence a wife holds — either to build or to tear down her home.

INTERPRETATION

The wise wife recognises that her words, attitudes, and decisions carry weight. She can nurture life or sow destruction. Her influence is subtle yet powerful, shaping the atmosphere of her home. God calls wives to be intentional builders, creating homes of peace, love, and faith.

CORRELATION

- Proverbs 31:26 — She opens her mouth with wisdom.
- Joshua 24:15 — As for me and my house, we will serve the Lord.
- Titus 2:4–5 — Teach the young women to love their husbands and children.

APPLICATION

Speak life-giving words over your home this week.

Identify one way you can build up your husband and family practically.

Prayer

Lord, help me to be a wise builder in my home. May my influence reflect Your wisdom and create an atmosphere of love and faith. Amen.

Journaling Prompts

- *How have my words influenced the atmosphere of my home recently?*
- *What intentional step can I take this week to build up rather than tear down?*

WEEK 9

Strength in Submission

*"Wives, submit to your own husbands,
as to the Lord."*

EPHESIANS 5:22 (NKJV)

OBSERVATION

Paul exhorts wives to submit to their husbands as an act of devotion to the Lord.

INTERPRETATION

Submission does not mean inferiority or silence. The Greek word *hypotasso* means to align under in order, much like soldiers in formation. It is voluntary, purposeful, and rooted in love. Submission to one's husband is ultimately an expression of submission to Christ, trusting His design for marriage.

CORRELATION

- Colossians 3:18 — Wives, submit to your husbands, as is fitting in the Lord.
- 1 Peter 3:5–6 — Holy women of old trusted God and submitted to their husbands.
- Philippians 2:5–7 — Christ Himself submitted in humility.

APPLICATION

Pray for the grace to align willingly with your husband's leadership.

Look for one way to support his decisions this week, trusting God's guidance.

PRAYER

Lord, teach me the beauty of submission. Help me to honour my husband as unto You, with humility and faith. Amen.

JOURNALING PROMPTS

- *How do I currently view submission in my marriage?*
- *What steps can I take to embrace submission as strength rather than weakness?*

WEEK 10

The Wife's Prayer Power

"The effective, fervent prayer of a righteous man avails much."

JAMES 5:16 (NKJV)

OBSERVATION

Prayer is a wife's hidden weapon, shaping her marriage and family in unseen but powerful ways.

INTERPRETATION

James teaches that fervent, faith-filled prayer is effective. A praying wife intercedes for her husband, children, and household. She shifts atmospheres, breaks chains, and invites God's will into her family. Her prayers are investments with eternal returns.

CORRELATION

- 1 Samuel 1:27 — Hannah prayed for this child, and the Lord granted her petition.
- Luke 18:1 — Men ought always to pray and not lose heart.
- Philippians 4:6 — In everything by prayer and supplication, make your requests known to God.

APPLICATION

Dedicate specific time this week to pray over your husband's work, health, and spiritual walk.

Start or strengthen a family prayer routine.

Prayer

Lord, make me a praying wife who stands in the gap. Let my prayers be fervent, effectual, and full of faith. Amen.

Journaling Prompts

- *What specific areas in my marriage need prayer covering?*
- *How can I cultivate consistency in my prayer life?*

WEEK 11

Hospitality from the Heart: Making Room for Grace

"Do not forget to entertain strangers; some have unwittingly entertained angels."

HEBREWS 13:2

OBSERVATION

Hospitality is a ministry of welcome, not perfection. It is love made visible through kindness.

INTERPRETATION

True hospitality opens both door and heart. When we welcome others with joy, God's peace fills the room. A wife who practises warmth and inclusion makes her home a sanctuary of grace.

CORRELATION

- Romans 12:13 — Practice hospitality.
- 1 Peter 4:9 — Offer hospitality without grumbling.
- Luke 10:38–42 — Mary and Martha welcomed Jesus.

APPLICATION

Invite someone into your home or share a meal.

Show kindness to a neighbour or family member.

PRAYER

Lord, fill my home with Your love and peace. May my welcome reflect Your heart. Amen.

JOURNALING PROMPTS

- *What small act of hospitality can I offer this week?*
- *How does God use my openness to bless others?*

WEEK 12

The Wife's Tongue

*"She opens her mouth
with wisdom, and on her tongue
is the law of kindness."*

PROVERBS 31:26 (NKJV)

OBSERVATION

Words have power — to heal, to build, or to destroy.

INTERPRETATION

A godly wife's speech is marked by wisdom and kindness. Her words nurture trust, build her husband's confidence, and shape the spiritual climate of her home. By yielding her tongue to God, she becomes a wellspring of life and encouragement.

CORRELATION

- Proverbs 18:21 — Death and life are in the power of the tongue.
- Colossians 4:6 — Let your speech be always with grace.
- James 3:9–10 — With the tongue we bless God and curse men — this should not be.

APPLICATION

Speak one intentional word of encouragement to your husband daily this week.

Replace negative or critical speech with affirmations of faith.

PRAYER

Lord, let Your wisdom and kindness guide my tongue. May my words bring life and encouragement to my home. Amen.

JOURNALING PROMPTS

- *What patterns of speech do I need to surrender to God?*
- *How can I use my words this week to build rather than tear down?*

WEEK 13

Faith that Stands: Trusting God Through Every Season

"Blessed is she who believed..."

LUKE 1:45

OBSERVATION

Mary trusted God beyond what she could see. Faith stands when sight fades.

INTERPRETATION

Faith that stands is quiet confidence in God's promise. It waits with worship, believing His Word over fear. Such faith strengthens marriages and steadies families through uncertainty.

CORRELATION

- Hebrews 11:1 — Faith is the substance of things hoped for.
- Mark 11:24 — Believe that you receive when you pray.
- Habakkuk 3:17–18 — Yet I will rejoice in the Lord.

APPLICATION

Declare one promise daily.

Turn every worry into praise.

Prayer

Lord, anchor my faith in You.
Help me stand firm through every season.
Amen.

Journaling Prompts

- *What promise am I believing for?*
- *How has faith shaped my past victories?*

WEEK 14

The Wife's Diligence

*"She watches over the ways
of her household, and does not
eat the bread of idleness."*

PROVERBS 31:27 (NKJV)

OBSERVATION

The Proverbs 31 woman models diligence in overseeing her household with care and intentionality.

INTERPRETATION

Diligence is not busyness, but purposeful stewardship. A diligent wife is attentive, wise, and faithful in managing her responsibilities. Her diligence builds trust and stability in her home, reflecting God's watchful care.

CORRELATION

- Colossians 3:23 — Whatever you do, do it heartily, as to the Lord.
- Proverbs 10:4 — The hand of the diligent makes rich.
- 1 Timothy 5:14 — Manage the household well.

APPLICATION

Choose one area of your household to improve or organise this week intentionally.

Approach your daily responsibilities as an act of worship to God.

Prayer

Lord, give me diligence to steward my home well. Help me to balance work and rest, honouring You in all I do. Amen.

Journaling Prompts

- *In what areas am I tempted toward idleness or distraction?*
- *How can I embrace diligence without becoming overwhelmed?*

WEEK 15

The Wife's Joy

"The joy of the Lord is your strength."
NEHEMIAH 8:10 (NKJV)

OBSERVATION

Joy is not circumstantial but rooted in the Lord. It gives strength to endure and thrive in every season.

INTERPRETATION

The Hebrew word for joy (*chedvah*) here is linked to delight in God's presence. A joyful wife creates an atmosphere of life and encouragement in her home. Her joy, rooted in Christ, becomes a testimony of God's sustaining grace even in trials.

CORRELATION

- Psalm 16:11 — In Your presence is fullness of joy.
- John 15:11 — That My joy may remain in you, and that your joy may be complete.
- Habakkuk 3:17–18 — I will rejoice in the Lord, I will joy in the God of my salvation.

APPLICATION

Practice gratitude daily by writing down three things you are thankful for.

Share joy with your family through laughter, kindness, or celebration this week.

Prayer

Lord, fill me with Your joy that strengthens and sustains me. Let my joy overflow and influence my home. Amen.

Journaling Prompts

- *What steals my joy most often, and how can I guard against it?*
- *How can I practically express joy in my marriage and family this week?*

WEEK 16

The Wife's Endurance

"Let us not grow weary while doing good, for in due season we shall reap if we do not lose heart."

GALATIANS 6:9 (NKJV)

OBSERVATION

Paul encourages perseverance, assuring believers that faithfulness will bear fruit in due time.

INTERPRETATION

Endurance is a vital quality in marriage and family life. Challenges will come, but a wife who endures with faith and hope becomes a stabilising force in her home. Her perseverance testifies to God's sustaining grace.

CORRELATION

- James 1:12 — Blessed is the one who perseveres under trial.
- Romans 5:3–4 — Suffering produces perseverance, character, and hope.
- Hebrews 10:36 — You need endurance to receive the promise.

APPLICATION

Commit to one act of goodness this week without expecting immediate results.

Encourage your husband or children to persevere in an area where they are struggling.

Prayer

Lord, grant me endurance to remain faithful in all You have called me to. Strengthen me not to lose heart, but to trust Your timing. Amen.

Journaling Prompts

- *Where am I most tempted to give up?*
- *How can I renew endurance through God's Word and prayer?*

WEEK 17

The Wife's Nurturing Heart

*"But we were gentle among you,
just as a nursing mother
cherishes her own children."*

1 THESSALONIANS 2:7 (NKJV)

OBSERVATION

Paul uses the image of a mother's nurture to describe his ministry. This reflects the tender, caring nature God entrusts to wives and mothers.

INTERPRETATION

Nurturing is more than providing care — it is cherishing. It is the intentional cultivation of life, growth, and well-being in others. A wife's nurturing heart mirrors God's compassion and provides stability and encouragement to her family.

CORRELATION

- Isaiah 66:13 — As a mother comforts her child, so will I comfort you.
- Proverbs 31:15 — She provides food for her household.
- Titus 2:4 — Encourage the young women to love their husbands and children.

APPLICATION

Look for one opportunity this week to intentionally nurture your husband or children emotionally or spiritually.

Speak words of comfort and encouragement to someone in your household.

Prayer

Lord, give me a nurturing heart that reflects Your love. Help me to cherish and build up those You have placed in my care. Amen.

Journaling Prompts

- *In what ways do I currently nurture my husband and family?*
- *How can I grow in cherishing rather than simply providing?*

WEEK 18

The Wife's Stewardship

"Moreover, it is required in stewards that one be found faithful."

1 CORINTHIANS 4:2 (NKJV)

OBSERVATION

Paul emphasises faithfulness as the chief requirement of stewardship. Wives are entrusted with much — their homes, resources, relationships, and influence.

INTERPRETATION

Stewardship means managing what belongs to God with wisdom and accountability. A faithful wife views her household not as her possession but as God's assignment. Her faithfulness in stewardship reflects her devotion to the Lord.

CORRELATION

- Luke 16:10 — Whoever is faithful in little will also be faithful in much.
- Proverbs 27:23 — Be diligent to know the state of your flocks.
- Matthew 25:21 — Well done, good and faithful servant.

APPLICATION

Evaluate one area of stewardship (time, finances, relationships) and commit it to God in prayer.

Take a small step this week to steward resources more faithfully.

Prayer

Lord, help me to be a faithful steward of all You have entrusted to me. May my management of resources, time, and relationships bring You glory. Amen.

Journaling Prompts

- *What has God entrusted me with that I need to steward more carefully?*
- *How does faithfulness in stewardship reflect my devotion to Christ?*

WEEK 19

The Wife's Encouragement

"Therefore, comfort each other and edify one another, just as you also are doing."

1 THESSALONIANS 5:11 (NKJV)

OBSERVATION

Encouragement is the ministry of building others up through words, presence, and prayer.

INTERPRETATION

The Greek word *parakaleo* means to come alongside, comfort, and strengthen. A wife's encouragement can breathe life into her husband and children. She becomes an instrument of hope, lifting burdens and pointing to God's promises.

CORRELATION

- Hebrews 10:24–25 — Encourage one another, especially as you see the Day approaching.
- Proverbs 12:25 — A good word makes the heart glad.
- Acts 4:36 — Barnabas was called the 'son of encouragement.'

APPLICATION

Speak a word of encouragement to your husband each day this week.

Identify someone in your community who needs encouragement and reach out to them.

Prayer

Lord, make me an encourager who builds others up. Let my words and presence point my family to Your strength and promises. Amen.

Journaling Prompts

- *How often do I intentionally encourage my husband and children?*
- *What hinders me from speaking encouragement more freely?*

W E E K 20

The Wife's Generosity

"She extends her hand to the poor, yes, she reaches out her hands to the needy."

PROVERBS 31:20 (NKJV)

OBSERVATION

Generosity is a mark of godliness. The Proverbs 31 wife demonstrates compassion through open hands and a willing heart.

INTERPRETATION

A generous wife reflects the heart of God, who gives abundantly. Her generosity blesses not only her family but also those beyond her home. She becomes a channel of God's provision and kindness to the world.

CORRELATION

- 2 Corinthians 9:7 — God loves a cheerful giver.
- Acts 20:35 — It is more blessed to give than to receive.
- Isaiah 58:10 — If you extend your soul to the hungry, your light will rise in the darkness.

APPLICATION

Find one way to practice generosity this week (time, resources, kindness).

Encourage your family to join you in an act of giving.

Prayer

Lord, make me a generous woman who reflects Your open hand. Use me to bless others and extend Your love. Amen.

Journaling Prompts

- *How do I currently practice generosity within and beyond my home?*
- *What step can I take to grow in cheerful giving?*

WEEK 21

Compassion that Heals: Reflecting Christ's Tender Heart

"Be tenderhearted, be courteous."

1 PETER 3:8

OBSERVATION

Compassion moves love from feeling to action.

INTERPRETATION

A compassionate wife mirrors Jesus' mercy. Her gentleness softens conflict and her empathy restores safety. Compassion is power wrapped in kindness—it heals quietly but deeply.

CORRELATION

- Colossians 3:12 — Clothe yourselves with compassion.
- Psalm 145:9 — The Lord's mercies are over all His works.
- Matthew 9:36 — Jesus was moved with compassion.

APPLICATION

Listen before speaking.

Comfort one who feels unseen.

Prayer

Lord, fill me with compassion that heals.
Let Your tenderness shape my home.
Amen.

Journaling Prompts

- *Who needs compassion from me today?*
- *How can gentleness change my relationships?*

WEEK 22

The Wife's Hope

*"Rejoicing in hope,
patient in tribulation,
continuing steadfastly in prayer."*

ROMANS 12:12 (NKJV)

OBSERVATION

Hope sustains the soul during challenges and anchors the heart in God's promises.

INTERPRETATION

Paul instructs believers to rejoice in hope — a joy rooted not in present circumstances but in the certainty of God's future. A hopeful wife uplifts her family, reminding them of God's faithfulness and strengthening them during trials.

CORRELATION

- Hebrews 6:19 — We have this hope as an anchor for the soul.
- Psalm 71:14 — But I will hope continually and praise You more and more.
- Jeremiah 29:11 — I know the plans I have for you, declares the Lord, plans to give you hope and a future.

APPLICATION

Share a testimony of God's faithfulness with your family this week.

Create a habit of declaring hopeful Scriptures over your home.

Prayer

Lord, fill my heart with hope that anchors me in You. Let my hope shine in my home and encourage my family. Amen.

Journaling Prompts

- *What situations in my life currently test my hope?*
- *How can I cultivate a perspective of hope rather than despair?*

WEEK 23

The Wife's Faithfulness

"A faithful man will abound with blessings, but he who hastens to be rich will not go unpunished."

PROVERBS 28:20 (NKJV)

OBSERVATION

Faithfulness is consistency in devotion, duty, and trustworthiness. It is a foundation for blessing.

INTERPRETATION

A faithful wife models steadfastness in her love, words, and actions. Her dependability builds trust in her marriage and stability in her home. Faithfulness is not perfection but reliability anchored in God's grace.

CORRELATION

- Lamentations 3:22–23 — Great is Your faithfulness.
- Matthew 25:23 — Well done, good and faithful servant.
- Galatians 5:22 — The fruit of the Spirit includes faithfulness.

APPLICATION

Evaluate one area where you can grow in consistency (devotion, encouragement, stewardship).

Affirm your commitment to your husband in a specific way this week.

Prayer

Lord, make me a faithful wife who reflects Your steadfast love. Strengthen me to remain consistent in my devotion and service. Amen.

Journaling Prompts

- *What does faithfulness look like practically in my marriage?*
- *Where do I need God's help to grow in consistency?*

WEEK 24

Gratitude in Every Season: Seeing God's Hand

"In everything give thanks."

1 THESSALONIANS 5:18

OBSERVATION

Gratitude shifts focus from lack to abundance.

INTERPRETATION

Thankfulness in every season keeps the heart light and the home joyful. A grateful wife turns ordinary days into worship and invites God's presence into her routines.

CORRELATION

- Colossians 3:17 — Do everything giving thanks.
- Psalm 100:4 — Enter His gates with thanksgiving.
- Philippians 4:6 — With thanksgiving, make your requests known.

APPLICATION

Write three blessings daily.

Express thanks aloud to your family.

Prayer

Lord, fill me with gratitude that sees Your hand in all things. Let thankfulness bring peace to our home. Amen.

Journaling Prompts

- *What am I grateful for today?*
- *How can gratitude shape my attitude?*

WEEK 25

Wisdom that Builds: Guiding with Discernment and Grace

"The wise woman builds her house."

PROVERBS 14:1

OBSERVATION

Wisdom applies truth in love.

INTERPRETATION

A wise wife listens to God before acting. Her words plant peace; her discernment shapes harmony. Wisdom is more than knowledge—it's divine perspective in daily choices.

CORRELATION

- James 1:5 — Ask God for wisdom.
- Proverbs 3:13 — Happy is she who finds wisdom.
- Colossians 3:16 — Let the word of Christ dwell in you richly.

APPLICATION

Pause before reacting.

Pray before deciding.

Prayer

Lord, give me wisdom to build with grace. Let my words bring peace, not pressure. Amen.

Journaling Prompts

- *What decision needs Your wisdom?*
- *How can I build, not break, today?*

WEEK 26

The Peacemaker's Presence: Cultivating Calm at Home

"Blessed are the peacemakers."

MATTHEW 5:9

OBSERVATION

Peace is not silence—it's Spirit-led calm.

INTERPRETATION

A peacemaker invites harmony where tension lives. Her presence quiets storms because her heart is ruled by Christ's peace. Calm spreads faster than conflict.

CORRELATION

- Colossians 3:15 — Let the peace of Christ rule your heart.
- Romans 12:18 — Live peaceably with all.
- Isaiah 26:3 — God keeps the steadfast mind in perfect peace.

APPLICATION

Respond with gentleness when frustrated.

Create peaceful moments of rest or prayer at home.

Prayer

Lord, make me a vessel of Your peace. Let calm flow from my heart into every room. Amen.

Journaling Prompts

- *What stirs tension in me?*
- *How can I sow peace this week?*

WEEK 27

The Wife's Respect

"Nevertheless let each one of you in particular so love his own wife as himself, and let the wife see that she respects her husband."

EPHESIANS 5:33 (NKJV)

OBSERVATION

Respect is the foundation of a wife's ministry to her husband.

INTERPRETATION

Paul emphasises that while husbands are commanded to love, wives are called to respect. Respect means honouring, affirming, and esteeming one's husband. A wife's respect breathes life into her husband's leadership and strengthens the marriage bond.

CORRELATION

- 1 Peter 3:1–2 — Wives, be submissive so that even without words, they may be won by conduct.
- Proverbs 31:11 — The heart of her husband safely trusts her.
- Romans 12:10 — Outdo one another in showing honour.

APPLICATION

Affirm one specific quality you respect in your husband this week.

Practice speaking respectfully even in disagreement.

Prayer

Lord, help me to respect my husband as unto You. May my words and actions affirm his value and strengthen our marriage. Amen.

Journaling Prompts

- *How do I currently show respect to my husband?*
- *What changes can I make to deepen respect in my marriage?*

WEEK 28

The Wife's Courage

*"Be strong and of good courage;
do not be afraid, nor be dismayed,
for the Lord your God
is with you wherever you go."*

JOSHUA 1:9 (NKJV)

OBSERVATION

Courage is the choice to trust God in the face of fear and uncertainty.

INTERPRETATION

Joshua was commanded to be strong and courageous because God's presence was with him. A courageous wife faces life's challenges with confidence in God's faithfulness. Her courage encourages her family to trust God boldly.

CORRELATION

- Psalm 27:1 — The Lord is my light and my salvation; whom shall I fear?
- 2 Timothy 1:7 — God has not given us a spirit of fear, but of power, love, and a sound mind.
- Deuteronomy 31:6 — Be strong and of good courage; He will not leave you nor forsake you.

APPLICATION

Face one fear this week by declaring God's promises over it.

Model courage before your family by choosing faith over fear.

Prayer

Lord, fill me with courage to trust You in every circumstance. Let my strength inspire faith in my family. Amen.

Journaling Prompts

- *What fears hold me back from fully trusting God?*
- *How can I show courage in my marriage and home this week?*

W E E K 29

The Wife's Service

"Through love serve one another."
GALATIANS 5:13 (NKJV)

OBSERVATION

Paul exhorts believers to express their freedom in Christ through loving service.

INTERPRETATION

A wife's service, motivated by love, strengthens her marriage and blesses her household. Service is not drudgery but an act of devotion that reflects Christ's servant-heart. It transforms ordinary tasks into sacred ministry.

CORRELATION

- Mark 10:45 — The Son of Man came not to be served, but to serve.
- John 13:14–15 — As I have washed your feet, you also ought to wash one another's feet.
- Philippians 2:3–4 — In humility, value others above yourselves.

APPLICATION

Perform one act of service for your husband without being asked.

Look for opportunities to serve your family with joy and humility.

Prayer

Lord, give me a servant's heart like Christ. May my service be marked by love and bring glory to You. Amen.

Journaling Prompts

- *Do I view my service as a burden or as worship?*
- *How can I cultivate joy in serving my family this week?*

WEEK 30

Forgiveness that Frees: Healing Through Grace

"Forgive one another, as God forgave you."

EPHESIANS 4:32

OBSERVATION

Forgiveness frees hearts and restores love.

INTERPRETATION

To forgive is to trust God with justice. A forgiving wife invites healing, not revenge. Her grace opens the way for reconciliation and joy.

CORRELATION

- Colossians 3:13 — Forgive as the Lord forgave you.
- Matthew 6:14 — If you forgive, your Father will forgive you.
- Psalm 103:12 — He removes our sins far away.

APPLICATION

Release one hurt in prayer.

Replace resentment with kindness.

Prayer

Lord, free me through forgiveness.
Let Your mercy flow in my home. Amen.

Journaling Prompts

- *Who do I need to release today?*
- *How does forgiveness renew peace?*

WEEK 31

Patience Perfected: Waiting with Faith and Love

"Let patience have its perfect work."

JAMES 1:4

OBSERVATION

Patience matures faith and reveals love.

INTERPRETATION

Waiting tests trust. A patient wife believes that God's timing brings better fruit than rushing ever could. Patience is love stretched across time, choosing grace instead of complaint.

CORRELATION

- Romans 12:12 — Patient in tribulation, steadfast in prayer.
- Galatians 6:9 — Do not grow weary; you'll reap in due time.
- Colossians 3:12 — Clothe yourselves with patience.

APPLICATION

Pause before reacting.

Thank God for unseen progress.

Prayer

Lord, grow patience in me.
Teach me to wait with faith and love.
Amen.

Journaling Prompts

- *Where am I rushing ahead of God?*
- *What does patient love look like in my home?*

WEEK 32

The Wife's Prayer

"Pray without ceasing."

1 THESSALONIANS 5:17 (NKJV)

OBSERVATION

Prayer is the lifeline of a believer — continual communion with God.

INTERPRETATION

A praying wife covers her home with God's presence and power. Her intercession shapes the spiritual atmosphere of her family and invites divine intervention. Prayer is not limited to words but is a lifestyle of dependence on God.

CORRELATION

- Philippians 4:6 — By prayer and supplication, with thanksgiving, let your requests be made known to God.
- James 5:16 — The effective, fervent prayer of a righteous person avails much.
- Luke 18:1 — Men always ought to pray and not lose heart.

APPLICATION

Set aside intentional time to pray for your husband and children this week.

Create a list of prayer points for your family and pray over them daily.

Prayer

Lord, make me a woman of prayer whose heart beats in constant communion with You. Cover my home with Your presence and power. Amen.

Journaling Prompts

- *How consistent is my prayer life for my marriage and family?*
- *What practical steps can I take to grow in unceasing prayer?*

W E E K 33

The Wife's Hospitality

"Do not forget to entertain strangers, for by so doing some have unwittingly entertained angels."

HEBREWS 13:2 (NKJV)

OBSERVATION

Hospitality is the open-hearted practice of welcoming others and making them feel at home.

INTERPRETATION

A hospitable wife reflects God's love by creating a warm and welcoming atmosphere in her home. Hospitality extends beyond entertaining; it is about sharing God's kindness and building relationships that glorify Him.

CORRELATION

- 1 Peter 4:9 — Be hospitable to one another without grumbling.
- Romans 12:13 — Practice hospitality.
- Genesis 18:2–3 — Abraham welcomed strangers and received God's blessing.

APPLICATION

Invite someone into your home or share a meal with a neighbour this week.

Practice small acts of hospitality within your own family through warmth and kindness.

Prayer

Lord, make my home a place of welcome and refuge. May my hospitality reflect Your love and draw others to You. Amen.

Journaling Prompts

- *How can I cultivate hospitality in simple, everyday ways?*
- *Who is God calling me to welcome into my home or life this week?*

WEEK 34

The Wife's Humility

"Humble yourselves in the sight of the Lord, and He will lift you up."

JAMES 4:10 (NKJV)

OBSERVATION

Humility is the posture of recognising our dependence on God and valuing others above ourselves.

INTERPRETATION

A humble wife avoids pride and selfish ambition. She serves her family with gentleness and honours God by walking in meekness. Her humility becomes a source of strength, enabling her to handle conflicts with grace and prioritise unity.

CORRELATION

- Philippians 2:3 — In humility consider others better than yourselves.
- Micah 6:8 — Walk humbly with your God.
- 1 Peter 5:6 — Humble yourselves under the mighty hand of God.

APPLICATION

Practice humility in your words by listening more than speaking this week.

Serve your husband or family in one unnoticed way without seeking recognition.

PRAYER

Lord, clothe me with humility that reflects Christ's example. Help me to serve others selflessly and walk in dependence on You. Amen.

JOURNALING PROMPTS

- *Where do I struggle most with pride in my marriage or family life?*
- *How can I intentionally walk in humility this week?*

WEEK 35

The Wife's Perseverance

*"And let us not grow weary
while doing good, for in due season
we shall reap if we do not lose heart."*

GALATIANS 6:9 (NKJV)

OBSERVATION

Perseverance is steady persistence in doing good, despite challenges or discouragement.

INTERPRETATION

A persevering wife does not give up when life is hard. She continues to sow love, faith, and hope, trusting God for the harvest. Her endurance inspires her family and strengthens her marriage through trials.

CORRELATION

- Romans 5:3–4 — Tribulation produces perseverance; perseverance, character; and character, hope.
- James 1:12 — Blessed is the one who perseveres under trial.
- Hebrews 12:1 — Run with endurance the race that is set before us.

APPLICATION

Identify one area where you are tempted to give up and commit it to God in prayer.

Encourage your husband or children not to lose heart in their struggles.

Prayer

Lord, strengthen me to persevere in doing good. Help me to endure with faith, knowing that You will bring a harvest in due season. Amen.

Journaling Prompts

- *Where in my marriage or family life do I need perseverance most?*
- *How does remembering God's promises fuel my endurance?*

WEEK 36

The Wife's Faith

"Without faith it is impossible to please Him, for he who comes to God must believe that He is, and that He is a rewarder of those who diligently seek Him."

HEBREWS 11:6 (NKJV)

OBSERVATION

Faith is trusting God's character and promises, even when circumstances seem uncertain.

INTERPRETATION

A faithful wife pleases God by relying on His Word and promises. Her faith strengthens her marriage by creating stability and inspiring her family to trust God as well. She becomes a witness to God's reliability and goodness.

CORRELATION

- 2 Corinthians 5:7 — For we walk by faith, not by sight.
- Mark 11:22 — Have faith in God.
- Matthew 17:20 — If you have faith as a mustard seed, nothing will be impossible for you.

APPLICATION

Write down one promise of God and declare it daily over your marriage.

Take a step of faith in an area you've been hesitant about.

PRAYER

Lord, deepen my faith so that I may walk in confidence in Your promises. Let my trust in You strengthen my family and glorify Your name. Amen.

JOURNALING PROMPTS

- *How strong is my faith when life's challenges arise?*
- *What step of faith is God calling me to take this week?*

WEEK 37

The Wife's Kindness

"And be kind to one another, tenderhearted, forgiving one another, even as God in Christ forgave you."

EPHESIANS 4:32 (NKJV)

OBSERVATION

Kindness is love expressed through gentle words and helpful deeds.

INTERPRETATION

A kind wife nurtures her family by choosing gentleness over harshness and generosity over selfishness. Her kindness reflects the heart of Christ, creating a safe and loving environment within her home.

CORRELATION

- Proverbs 31:26 — She opens her mouth with wisdom, and on her tongue is the law of kindness.
- Colossians 3:12 — Clothe yourselves with kindness, humility, gentleness, and patience.
- Titus 3:4 — The kindness of God appeared in Christ Jesus.

APPLICATION

Do one unexpected act of kindness for your husband or children this week.

Use words that uplift and encourage, especially in moments of stress.

Prayer

Lord, clothe me with kindness that reflects Your love. Let my words and actions nurture peace in my home. Amen.

Journaling Prompts

- *In what ways do I show kindness in my marriage?*
- *How can I grow in practical expressions of kindness this week?*

WEEK 38

The Wife's Joy

*"Rejoice in the Lord always.
Again I will say, rejoice!"*

PHILIPPIANS 4:4 (NKJV)

OBSERVATION

Joy is a fruit of the Spirit that transcends circumstances because it is rooted in God.

INTERPRETATION

A joyful wife brings light into her home, lifting burdens with her attitude and faith. Her joy is not dependent on external conditions but springs from her relationship with Christ, inspiring hope in her family.

CORRELATION

- Nehemiah 8:10 — The joy of the Lord is your strength.
- John 15:11 — These things I have spoken to you, that My joy may remain in you.
- Romans 15:13 — May the God of hope fill you with all joy and peace in believing.

APPLICATION

Choose to rejoice in one difficult situation this week as an act of faith.

Share moments of laughter and joy with your family intentionally.

Prayer

Lord, fill my heart with joy that overflows into my home. Let my delight in You be a source of strength and encouragement to my family. Amen.

Journaling Prompts

- *What robs me of joy most often?*
- *How can I cultivate joy as a daily choice?*

W E E K 39

The Wife's Integrity

"The integrity of the upright will guide them, but the perversity of the unfaithful will destroy them."

PROVERBS 11:3 (NKJV)

OBSERVATION

Integrity is living truthfully and consistently according to God's Word.

INTERPRETATION

A wife of integrity builds trust in her home through honesty, faithfulness, and consistency. Her life becomes a compass for her family, pointing them toward righteousness and stability.

CORRELATION

- Psalm 25:21 — Let integrity and uprightness preserve me.
- Proverbs 20:7 — The righteous man walks in his integrity; his children are blessed after him.
- Job 2:3 — Job still holds fast to his integrity.

APPLICATION

Speak truthfully in all situations this week, even when it is difficult.

Model consistency in your values for your family to follow.

Prayer

Lord, shape me into a woman of integrity. Let my words and actions align with Your truth and bring honour to You. Amen.

Journaling Prompts

- *Do my actions match the values I profess?*
- *How can I strengthen integrity in my marriage and family life?*

WEEK 40

The Wife's Obedience

*"If you love Me,
keep My commandments."*

JOHN 14:15 (NKJV)

OBSERVATION

Obedience is the outward expression of inward love for God.

INTERPRETATION

A wife who walks in obedience honours God first, and in doing so blesses her family. Her obedience demonstrates trust in God's wisdom and becomes a testimony of devotion and surrender.

CORRELATION

- 1 Samuel 15:22 — To obey is better than sacrifice.
- Deuteronomy 5:33 — Walk in obedience to all the Lord has commanded you.
- Luke 11:28 — Blessed are those who hear the word of God and keep it.

APPLICATION

Identify one command of God you've been neglecting and commit to obeying it this week.

Teach your family about obedience through your example.

PRAYER

Lord, help me to walk in loving obedience to Your Word. Let my surrender inspire faith and devotion in my home. Amen.

JOURNALING PROMPTS

- *What area of my life is God calling me to deeper obedience?*
- *How can I model joyful obedience before my family?*

WEEK 41

The Wife's Gratitude

*"In everything give thanks;
for this is the will of God
in Christ Jesus for you."*

1 THESSALONIANS 5:18 (NKJV)

OBSERVATION

Gratitude is the practice of recognising God's blessings and responding with thanksgiving.

INTERPRETATION

A grateful wife transforms her home by focusing on God's goodness rather than on complaints. Gratitude shifts the atmosphere, fosters contentment, and honours God in all circumstances.

CORRELATION

- Colossians 3:17 — Whatever you do, do all in the name of the Lord Jesus, giving thanks.
- Psalm 100:4 — Enter His gates with thanksgiving.
- Philippians 4:6 — With thanksgiving, let your requests be made known to God.

APPLICATION

Keep a gratitude journal this week, writing down three things daily.

Verbally thank your husband and family members for specific actions.

Prayer

Lord, give me a heart of gratitude that magnifies Your goodness and shifts the atmosphere of my home. Amen.

Journaling Prompts

- *What blessings am I overlooking in my daily life?*
- *How can I model gratitude before my family this week?*

WEEK 42

The Wife's Hope

*"Now may the God of hope
fill you with all joy and peace
in believing, that you may
abound in hope by the power
of the Holy Spirit."*

ROMANS 15:13 (NKJV)

OBSERVATION

Hope is a confident expectation rooted in God's promises.

INTERPRETATION

A hopeful wife anchors her family in the assurance of God's faithfulness. Her hope inspires resilience during trials and points her household toward God's plans.

CORRELATION

- Jeremiah 29:11 — I know the plans I have for you, plans to give you hope and a future.
- Hebrews 6:19 — This hope we have as an anchor of the soul.
- Psalm 42:11 — Hope in God, for I shall yet praise Him.

APPLICATION

Speak words of hope into one discouraging situation this week.

Encourage your husband and children by reminding them of God's promises.

Prayer

Lord, fill my heart with hope that overflows into my family. Anchor us in Your promises and strengthen us in every trial. Amen.

Journaling Prompts

- *Where do I need to place my hope back in God?*
- *How can I share hope with someone in my family this week?*

WEEK 43

The Wife's Faithfulness

"Moreover, it is required in stewards that one be found faithful."

1 CORINTHIANS 4:2 (NKJV)

OBSERVATION

Faithfulness is consistency in loyalty, devotion, and responsibility before God and others.

INTERPRETATION

A faithful wife is reliable in her commitments and steadfast in her love. Her faithfulness reflects God's covenant loyalty and becomes a foundation of trust in her marriage and family.

CORRELATION

- Proverbs 3:3 — Let love and faithfulness never leave you.
- Galatians 5:22 — The fruit of the Spirit is faithfulness.
- Matthew 25:23 — Well done, good and faithful servant.

APPLICATION

Identify one area in your marriage or family where you need to grow in consistency.

Commit to keeping one promise to your husband or children this week.

PRAYER

Lord, make me a faithful steward of the family You have entrusted to me. May my consistency reflect Your unchanging love. Amen.

JOURNALING PROMPTS

- *Am I reliable in fulfilling the commitments I make to my family?*
- *How can I reflect God's faithfulness more clearly this week?*

W E E K

The Wife's Love

"And above all these things put on love, which is the bond of perfection."

COLOSSIANS 3:14 (NKJV)

OBSERVATION

Love is the supreme virtue that binds all other qualities together.

INTERPRETATION

A loving wife mirrors God's nature by prioritising sacrificial love in her home. Her love is not merely emotional but active, demonstrated through patience, kindness, and service. Love perfects and unites her family in Christ.

CORRELATION

- 1 Corinthians 13:4–7 — Love is patient, love is kind.
- 1 John 4:7 — Let us love one another, for love is of God.
- Romans 13:10 — Love is the fulfilment of the law.

APPLICATION

Do one intentional act of sacrificial love for your husband or children this week.

Pray that God's love would overflow through you in all interactions.

PRAYER

Lord, fill me with Your love that binds everything together in harmony. Let my home be a reflection of Your perfect love. Amen.

JOURNALING PROMPTS

- *How can I deepen my expressions of love in my marriage?*
- *What does sacrificial love look like in my family this week?*

WEEK 45

The Wife's Peace

*"Blessed are the peacemakers,
for they shall be called sons of God."*
MATTHEW 5:9 (NKJV)

OBSERVATION

Peace is more than the absence of conflict; it is the presence of harmony rooted in Christ.

INTERPRETATION

A peace-making wife seeks reconciliation, avoids unnecessary strife, and creates an environment of calm in her home. Her peace reflects God's character and brings stability to her marriage and family.

CORRELATION

- Romans 12:18 — If it is possible, as much as depends on you, live peaceably with all men.
- Colossians 3:15 — Let the peace of Christ rule in your hearts.
- Isaiah 26:3 — You will keep him in perfect peace, whose mind is stayed on You.

APPLICATION

Choose peace over argument in one situation this week.

Pray for God's peace to rule over your family during tense moments.

PRAYER

Lord, make me a peacemaker in my marriage and home. Let Your peace rule in my heart and flow into every relationship. Amen.

JOURNALING PROMPTS

- *Do I contribute to peace or tension in my marriage?*
- *How can I practically cultivate peace in my family this week?*

WEEK 46

The Wife's Wisdom

"The wise woman builds her house, but the foolish pulls it down with her hands."

PROVERBS 14:1 (NKJV)

OBSERVATION

Wisdom is applying God's truth rightly in daily life.

INTERPRETATION

A wise wife strengthens her marriage and family by making choices rooted in God's Word. Her discernment prevents destruction and brings blessing to her household.

CORRELATION

- James 1:5 — If any of you lacks wisdom, let him ask of God.
- Proverbs 3:13 — Happy is the one who finds wisdom.
- Ecclesiastes 7:12 — Wisdom preserves those who have it.

APPLICATION

Pray for wisdom before making one major decision this week.

Share one insight from God's Word with your husband or children.

PRAYER

Lord, grant me wisdom from above to guide my words and actions. May my decisions build up my home and honour You. Amen.

JOURNALING PROMPTS

- *What recent decision requires me to seek God's wisdom?*
- *How am I actively building my house with wisdom daily?*

W E E K 47

The Wife's Contentment

"Now godliness with contentment is great gain."

1 TIMOTHY 6:6 (NKJV)

OBSERVATION

Contentment is resting in God's provision without striving for more than He intends.

INTERPRETATION

A content wife brings peace into her marriage and home by refusing envy or comparison. Her satisfaction in God's goodness prevents strife and cultivates joy within her family.

CORRELATION

- Philippians 4:11 — I have learned to be content in whatever the circumstances.
- Hebrews 13:5 — Be content with what you have, for God has said, 'I will never leave you.'
- Psalm 23:1 — The Lord is my shepherd; I shall not want.

APPLICATION

Resist comparison by thanking God for one specific blessing in your marriage.

Simplify one area of life to focus more on gratitude than gain.

PRAYER

Lord, teach me to rest in Your provision and to embrace contentment. May my heart overflow with gratitude and peace. Amen.

JOURNALING PROMPTS

- *Where am I tempted to compare my life or marriage to others?*
- *How can I practice gratitude as the pathway to contentment this week?*

W E E K 48

The Wife's Strength

*"She girds herself with strength,
and strengthens her arms."*

PROVERBS 31:17 (NKJV)

OBSERVATION

Strength in the Bible is both physical vitality and spiritual resilience from God.

INTERPRETATION

A strong wife endures trials, supports her husband, and provides stability for her family. Her strength comes from dependence on God and becomes a pillar of encouragement in her household.

CORRELATION

- Nehemiah 8:10 — The joy of the Lord is your strength.
- Isaiah 40:31 — Those who wait on the Lord shall renew their strength.
- Psalm 46:1 — God is our refuge and strength.

APPLICATION

Rely on God's strength to complete one challenging task this week.

Encourage your family by pointing them to God's sustaining power.

PRAYER

Lord, clothe me with Your strength for every task and trial. May I be a source of resilience and encouragement in my family. Amen.

JOURNALING PROMPTS

- *Do I rely on my own strength or God's strength in daily life?*
- *How can I demonstrate spiritual resilience in my home this week?*

W E E K 49

The Wife's Patience

*"But let patience have its perfect work,
that you may be perfect and
complete, lacking nothing."*

JAMES 1:4 (NKJV)

OBSERVATION

Patience is the Spirit-enabled ability to endure delay, hardship, or provocation without complaint.

INTERPRETATION

A patient wife reflects Christ's forbearance in her marriage and family. She chooses grace over irritation and endures difficulties with hope. Her patience nurtures unity and peace in her home.

CORRELATION

- Romans 12:12 — Rejoicing in hope, patient in tribulation, continuing steadfastly in prayer.
- Colossians 3:12 — Clothe yourselves with compassion, kindness, humility, gentleness, and patience.
- Ecclesiastes 7:8 — The patient in spirit is better than the proud in spirit.

APPLICATION

Pause and pray instead of reacting quickly in a stressful moment this week.

Extend patience intentionally to your husband or children in a challenging situation.

Prayer

Lord, grant me patience that reflects Your character. Help me to bear with others in love and trust in Your perfect timing. Amen.

Journaling Prompts

- *Where do I struggle most with impatience in my marriage or family life?*
- *How can I cultivate patience as an act of faith this week?*

W E E K 50

The Wife's Compassion

*"Finally, all of you be of one mind,
having compassion for one another;
love as brothers, be tenderhearted,
be courteous."*

1 PETER 3:8 (NKJV)

OBSERVATION

Compassion is heartfelt concern that moves us to care for the needs of others.

INTERPRETATION

A compassionate wife reflects Christ's mercy by being attentive to the struggles of her husband, children, and others. Her compassion brings comfort and healing, modelling the love of Christ within her home.

CORRELATION

- Colossians 3:12 — Put on tender mercies, kindness, humility, meekness, longsuffering.
- Psalm 145:9 — The Lord is good to all; His tender mercies are over all His works.
- Matthew 9:36 — Jesus was moved with compassion for the multitudes.

APPLICATION

Look for one opportunity to meet an emotional or physical need in your family this week.

Respond with compassion instead of criticism in a moment of conflict.

Prayer

Lord, fill me with Christ-like compassion. May I reflect Your mercy in my marriage, family, and community. Amen.

Journaling Prompts

- *When was the last time I truly showed compassion to my spouse or children?*
- *How can I grow in sensitivity to the needs of others?*

WEEK 51

The Wife's Forgiveness

*"And forgive us our debts,
as we forgive our debtors."*
MATTHEW 6:12 (NKJV)

OBSERVATION

Forgiveness is releasing others from the debt of their offences, as God has forgiven us.

INTERPRETATION

A forgiving wife mirrors the heart of Christ by refusing to hold grudges. Her forgiveness brings healing to relationships and models the grace of God to her family.

CORRELATION

- Ephesians 4:32 — Forgive one another, just as God in Christ forgave you.
- Mark 11:25 — When you stand praying, forgive if you have anything against anyone.
- Colossians 3:13 — Bear with each other and forgive whatever grievances you may have.

APPLICATION

Release one past hurt or resentment through prayer this week.

Verbally extend forgiveness to someone in your home, if needed.

Prayer

Lord, give me the grace to forgive as You have forgiven me. Heal any bitterness in my heart and restore unity in my relationships. Amen.

Journaling Prompts

- *Is there someone in my family I need to forgive right now?*
- *How can I practice forgiveness more quickly and freely in the future?*

WEEK 52

The Wife's Devotion

"But seek first the kingdom of God and His righteousness, and all these things shall be added to you."

MATTHEW 6:33 (NKJV)

OBSERVATION

Devotion is wholehearted dedication to God above all else.

INTERPRETATION

A devoted wife prioritises her relationship with God, which in turn enriches her marriage and family. Her devotion shapes her identity, guides her decisions, and inspires her family to pursue God wholeheartedly.

CORRELATION

- Psalm 63:1 — O God, You are my God; early will I seek You.
- Joshua 24:15 — As for me and my house, we will serve the Lord.
- Romans 12:11 — Be fervent in spirit, serving the Lord.

APPLICATION

Set aside dedicated time this week for prayer and Scripture reading.

Lead your family in one act of devotion, such as prayer or worship together.

PRAYER

Lord, deepen my devotion to You above all else. May my wholehearted pursuit of You transform my marriage and family. Amen.

JOURNALING PROMPTS

- *What distracts me most from prioritising God in my life?*
- *How can I lead my family in greater devotion to the Lord this week?*

OTHER BOOKS
BY THE AUTHOR

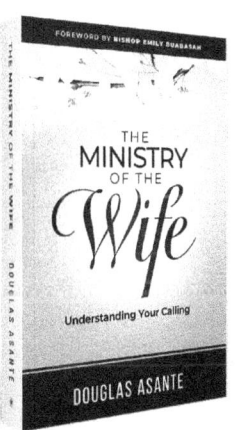

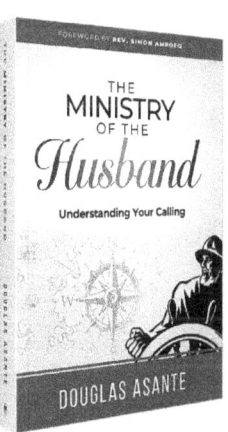

AVAILABLE ON
amazon   amazon kindle

www.dasante.org.uk

www.ingramcontent.com/pod-product-compliance
Lightning Source LLC
Chambersburg PA
CBHW021014090426
42738CB00007B/787